contents

introduction

Gathering good friends together with fabulous cocktails and nibbles is one of the most enjoyable ways of entertaining. Here you'll find all the food and drink ideas you will need to make your party a success, from margaritas and mojitos, to beef & stilton pies and caramelised onion & goats cheese quiches. Salute!

asparagus, tomato & goats cheese tarts

170g asparagus
125g cherry tomatoes
1 teaspoon finely grated
   lemon rind
1 tablespoon olive oil
¼ cup lightly packed fresh
   basil leaves, shredded finely
   (see page 110)
20 shortcrust or fillo pastry
   cases (see pages 108 & 109)
70g marinated goats cheese,
   drained

1 Trim asparagus; slice thinly. Boil, steam or microwave asparagus until tender; drain. Rinse under cold water; drain.
2 Halve tomatoes; cut into thin wedges.
3 Combine asparagus and tomatoes in medium bowl with rind, oil and half the basil.
4 Divide half the asparagus mixture into pastry cases; top with cheese, then remaining asparagus mixture. Sprinkle with remaining basil.

prep + cook time 25 minutes
makes 20
tip You can use fetta cheese in place of goats cheese.
Make-ahead tips
1 week Make pastry cases; store in an airtight container.
8 hours Prepare asparagus and tomatoes for asparagus mixture, cover, refrigerate separately.
Last Assemble tarts just before serving.

2 medium red capsicums (400g)
4 medium tomatoes (600g),
   halved
1 fresh long red chilli,
   halved lengthways
5 unpeeled cloves garlic
2 cups (500ml) chicken stock
basil pesto
1 cup loosely packed fresh
   basil leaves
1½ tablespoons finely grated
   parmesan cheese
1 tablespoon lemon juice
1 tablespoon roasted pine nuts
2 tablespoons olive oil

1 Preheat oven to 240°C/220°C fan-forced.
2 Quarter capsicums; discard seeds and membranes. Place quarters, skin-side up, on oiled oven tray with tomatoes, cut-side up, and chilli and garlic. Roast, uncovered, about 20 minutes or until capsicum skin blisters and blackens and vegetables are soft.
3 Cover vegetables with foil, stand 10 minutes; peel away skin.
4 Reserve one garlic clove for pesto. Blend vegetables and stock until smooth; strain.
5 Meanwhile, make basil pesto.
6 Reheat soup in medium saucepan. Divide soup into shot glasses; top each with tiny amount of pesto. Garnish with chilli curls.
basil pesto Blend reserved garlic, basil, cheese, juice and nuts until chopped. With motor operating, gradually add oil in a thin stream until smooth.

prep + cook time 55 minutes (+ standing)
serves 30
tips Use the most flavoursome tomatoes you can buy. A blender will make a fine-textured soup and pesto. Make chilli curls by slicing a long red chilli thinly lengthways. Place strips in iced water for about 10 minutes.
Make-ahead tips
1 month Make soup and pesto; freeze separately.
24 hours Thaw soup and pesto in refrigerator overnight.
Last Reheat soup. Pesto might need a little oil stirred through for a good consistency.

capsicum & tomato soup with basil pesto

pomegranate caipiroska

Cut ½ lime into quarters. Using muddler (see page 110), crush two lime wedges in cocktail shaker with 60ml vodka, 30ml sugar syrup (see page 112) and 20ml pomegranate juice. Add 1 cup ice cubes; shake vigorously. Strain into ice-filled 260ml old-fashioned glass; stir in 1 tablespoon pomegranate pulp. Garnish with remaining sliced lime wedges. **prep time** 5 minutes **serves** 1

cosmopolitan

Place 1 cup ice cubes, 45ml vodka, 30ml cointreau, 20ml cranberry juice and 10ml lime juice in cocktail shaker; shake vigorously. Strain into chilled 230ml martini glass. Garnish with strip orange rind made using a zester. **prep time** 5 minutes **serves** 1

parmesan scones with goats cheese & tapenade

1½ cups (225g) self-raising flour
30g butter
¼ cup (30g) finely grated
   parmesan cheese
¾ cup (180ml) buttermilk,
   approximately
180g goats cheese
bunch fresh flat-leaf parsley
tapenade
200g seeded black olives
1 tablespoon rinsed drained
   capers
1 clove garlic, quartered
½ cup coarsely chopped
   fresh flat-leaf parsley
5 drained anchovy fillets
1 tablespoon lemon juice
1 tablespoon olive oil

1 Preheat oven to 200°C/180°C fan-forced. Oil oven tray.
2 Sift flour into large bowl; rub in butter, then stir in parmesan. Using a knife, mix in enough buttermilk to make a soft dough.
3 Turn dough onto floured surface, knead lightly until smooth. Press dough out to 1.5cm thickness, cut out 30 x 3cm rounds.
4 Place scones, barely touching each other, on tray. Bake about 20 minutes. Turn scones onto wire rack, cover, cool.
5 Meanwhile, make tapenade.
6 Split scones in half, top each half with tapenade and goats cheese; top each with a parsley leaf.
tapenade Process ingredients until chopped coarsely.

prep + cook time 45 minutes
makes 60
tip Good quality tapenade is easy to buy if you don't want to make your own.
Make-ahead tips
1 month Freeze cooled baked scones wrapped in foil.
1 week Make tapenade, store in an airtight container, covered with a layer of olive oil; refrigerate.
Last Reheat frozen, foil-wrapped scones on oven tray, at 180°C/160°C fan-forced, for about 10 minutes. Assemble scones up to 30 minutes before serving; keep covered at room temperature.

60g butter
1 teaspoon mustard powder
½ teaspoon sweet paprika
½ teaspoon chilli powder
⅓ cup (50g) plain flour
1½ cups (375ml) milk
¾ cup (90g) coarsely grated
  gouda cheese
1 cup (100g) coarsely grated
  mozzarella cheese
4 green onions, chopped finely
¼ cup (35g) plain flour, extra
¾ cup (75g) packaged
  breadcrumbs
2 eggs
vegetable oil, for deep-frying
mint salsa
1 cup lightly packed fresh
  flat-leaf parsley leaves
½ cup lightly packed fresh
  mint leaves
3 teaspoons red wine vinegar
½ teaspoon white sugar
2 teaspoons rinsed drained
  baby capers
2 tablespoons olive oil

1 Melt butter in medium saucepan, stir in spices and flour; cook, stirring, over medium heat until mixture bubbles. Remove from heat, gradually stir in milk; stir over heat until mixture boils and thickens.
2 Remove pan from heat, stir in cheeses until smooth; stir in onion. Cover sauce, refrigerate about 3 hours or until firm.
3 Make mint salsa.
4 Place extra flour and breadcrumbs in separate medium shallow bowls. Beat eggs lightly in another medium shallow bowl. Drop teaspoonfuls of cheese sauce into flour, coat lightly; shake away excess. Dip in egg, then in breadcrumbs; place on tray. Cover; refrigerate 30 minutes.
5 Heat oil in wok or deep, wide saucepan to 180°C. Deep-fry fritters in batches until golden brown; drain on absorbent paper. Serve fritters with salsa.
mint salsa Blend or process ingredients until smooth.

prep + cook time 45 minutes (+ refrigeration)
makes 72
tip Make sure the oil for deep frying is very hot, only deep-fry the fritters for a few seconds, or they will break open.
Make-ahead tips
24 hours Prepare and crumb fritters; cover, refrigerate. Make mint salsa; cover, refrigerate.
Last Deep-fry fritters as close as possible to serving time.

oozy cheese fritters

zucchini, pea & fontina pasties

2 teaspoons olive oil
1 small brown onion (100g),
   chopped finely
2 medium zucchini (240g),
   grated coarsely
¾ cup (90g) frozen peas,
   thawed
¼ cup lightly packed fresh
   mint leaves, sliced finely
100g fontina cheese,
   cut into 5mm cubes
1 teaspoon finely grated
   lemon rind
1 egg yolk
1 tablespoon milk
hot water pastry
¾ cup (180ml) water
125g butter, chopped coarsely
3 cups (450g) plain flour
1 teaspoon salt
1 egg yolk

1 Preheat oven to 200°C/180°C fan-forced. Oil oven trays.
2 Heat oil in large frying pan, cook onion and zucchini over high heat until vegetables are softened slightly. Cool.
3 Stir peas, mint, cheese and rind into zucchini mixture.
4 Make hot water pastry.
5 Cut pastry in half, return one half to same bowl; cover with tea towel to keep warm. Roll other half of pastry as thinly as possible, on a floured surface into a round about 50cm in diameter.
6 Working quickly, cut out 8cm rounds from pastry, cover pastry with tea towel to prevent drying out while shaping each pasty. Place a rounded teaspoon of filling on each pastry round, fold in half and press edges together firmly. Place pasties on trays; brush with combined egg yolk and milk.
7 Bake pasties about 25 minutes, or until golden brown. Serve warm with minted yogurt.

hot water pastry Bring the water and butter to the boil in small saucepan. Meanwhile, sift flour and salt into large bowl. Make a well in the centre, add egg yolk; cover yolk with some of the flour. Pour boiling water mixture over the flour, stirring constantly with a knife until ingredients are combined. Knead pastry lightly and quickly on floured surface until smooth. Place pastry in bowl, cover with tea towel to keep warm.

prep + cook time 1 hour
makes 60
Make-ahead tips
1 month Freeze uncooked pastries in airtight containers.
Last To reheat: place frozen pasties on oven trays, cover loosely with foil, reheat at 200°C/180°C fan-forced for about 25 minutes.

340g asparagus, trimmed
250g haloumi cheese
lemony dressing
1 tablespoon rinsed drained
    baby capers, chopped finely
1 tablespoon olive oil
2 teaspoons finely grated
    lemon rind
1 tablespoon lemon juice
½ teaspoon white sugar

1 Make lemony dressing.
2 Cut asparagus into 3cm lengths. Boil, steam or microwave until barely tender; rinse under cold water, drain.
3 Cut haloumi into 1cm slices, then into 1cm x 3cm pieces. Thread one piece of asparagus, one piece of haloumi, then another piece of asparagus close together onto each toothpick.
4 Cook bites in large oiled frying pan over high heat about 30 seconds each side or until browned lightly.
5 Serve bites immediately, drizzled with dressing.
lemony dressing Place ingredients in a screw-top jar; shake well.

prep + cook time 55 minutes
makes 40
tip Use strong wooden toothpicks for this recipe or short pieces of bamboo skewers.
Make-ahead tips
8 hours Prepare asparagus and haloumi on toothpicks, ready for cooking; cover, refrigerate. Make dressing; refrigerate.
Last Cook bites as close to serving as possible as the haloumi will toughen as it cools.

haloumi & asparagus bites with lemony dressing

martini

Place 1 small rinsed seeded green olive and dash dry vermouth into chilled 120ml martini glass; swirl vermouth in glass to coat. Place 1 cup ice cubes and 45ml gin in cocktail shaker; shake vigorously. Strain into glass. **prep time** 5 minutes **serves** 1

vodka martini

Place 1 small rinsed seeded green olive and dash dry vermouth into chilled 120ml martini glass; swirl vermouth in glass to coat. Place 1 cup ice cubes and 45ml vodka in cocktail shaker; shake vigorously. Strain into glass. **prep time** 5 minutes **serves** 1

600g mixed mushrooms
2 tablespoons olive oil
40g butter
3 cloves garlic, crushed
3 sprigs fresh thyme
¼ cup finely grated
 parmesan cheese
2 tablespoons finely chopped
 fresh flat-leaf parsley
2 teaspoons worcestershire
 sauce
250g brioche
⅓ cup (80g) sour cream
2 tablespoons finely chopped
 fresh chives

1 Preheat oven to 150°C/130°C fan-forced.
2 Process mushrooms until chopped finely.
3 Heat oil and butter in large frying pan; cook garlic, thyme and mushrooms, stirring, until tender. Discard thyme stems. Stir in cheese, parsley and sauce.
4 Cut brioche into 1cm slices, toast both sides lightly in an electric toaster or under a preheated grill. Cut out 3.5cm rounds from brioche slices, place on oven tray; toast again in oven about 5 minutes or until crisp.
5 Place one teaspoon mushroom mixture on each toast, top with sour cream and chives.

prep + cook time 40 minutes
makes 48

tips Use whatever mushrooms you like: we used a combination of button, swiss brown and oyster mushrooms. Cook mushrooms until juices evaporate, so they don't make the brioche soggy.

Make-ahead tips

7 days Toast brioche rounds in oven to dry out, cool, store in an airtight container. Cook mushroom mixture, cool and freeze.

Last Thaw and reheat mushroom mixture by stirring over low heat in a large frying pan with a little extra butter or cream, or in the microwave oven. Assemble toasties just before serving.

mushroom toasties

onion & kumara pakoras with green chilli yogurt

2 cups (300g) chickpea
   (besan) flour
1 teaspoon ground turmeric
2 teaspoons ground cumin
½ teaspoon chilli powder
1 teaspoon baking powder
½ teaspoon salt
2 teaspoons kalonji seeds
2 medium brown onions (300g),
   quartered, sliced thinly
1 small uncooked kumara (250g),
   grated coarsely
1 fresh long green chilli,
   chopped finely
½ cup (125ml) water,
   approximately
vegetable oil, for deep-frying

green chilli yogurt
1½ cups (420g) greek-style
   yogurt
2 fresh long green chillies,
   seeded, chopped finely
2 tablespoons finely chopped
   coriander leaves
½ teaspoon ground cumin

1 Sift flour, turmeric, cumin, chilli, baking powder and salt into large bowl. Stir in seeds, onion, kumara and chilli. Gradually stir in enough water to make a thick batter
2 Make green chilli yogurt.
3 Heat oil in wok or deep wide saucepan; deep-fry rounded teaspoons of batter mixture, in batches, until browned. Drain on absorbent paper.
4 Serve pakoras hot, with yogurt.
green chilli yogurt Combine ingredients in medium bowl.

prep + cook time 35 minutes
makes 80
tip Batter will continue to thicken as it stands. If necessary, add a little water to thin it out.
Make-ahead tips
24 hours Prepare ingredients for pakoras; cover, refrigerate. Make the green chilli yogurt; cover, refrigerate.
Last Make batter and deep-fry pakoras just before serving.

24 quail eggs

za'atar

¼ cup sesame seeds

1½ teaspoons sumac

2 tablespoons fresh thyme
leaves

1 teaspoon sea salt

1 Make za'atar.
2 Place quail eggs in a single
layer in a wide saucepan.
Barely cover eggs with cold
water; cover pan. Bring to the
boil over high heat; remove
lid, boil eggs for 1½ minutes.
Drain eggs, rinse with cold
water. Crack the shell of each
egg, place eggs in a bowl of
cold water, shell eggs under
the water, remove each egg to
serving platter as you shell it.
3 Serve eggs warm with za'atar
for dipping.
za'atar Stir sesame seeds in
medium frying pan over medium
heat until browned lightly;
remove from pan to cool. Using
mortar and pestle, grind sumac,
thyme and salt until fine. Add
seeds, crush lightly.

prep + cook time 20 minutes
makes 24
tips Serve eggs with toothpicks
to make dipping easier. We like
to serve the eggs warm, but cold
is good too.
Make-ahead tips
1 week Make za'atar; store in
an airtight container.
Last Cook and shell eggs.

quail eggs with za'atar

sweet corn fritters with rocket puree

1 egg
½ cup (125ml) milk
1 cup (160g) corn kernels
½ small red capsicum (75g), roasted, chopped finely
½ small red onion (50g), chopped finely
1 tablespoon finely chopped fresh basil
½ cup (75g) self-raising flour
pinch bicarbonate of soda
½ cup (120g) sour cream

rocket puree
125g rocket
2 teaspoons olive oil

1 Make rocket puree.
2 Whisk egg and milk in large bowl, stir in vegetables and basil. Sift flour and soda over vegetable mixture, stir until combined.
3 Cook rounded teaspoonfuls vegetable mixture in large oiled frying pan, over medium heat, about 2 minutes each side or until fritters are browned.
4 Top each fritter with about ½ teaspoon each of sour cream and rocket puree. Serve fritters immediately.

rocket puree Bring a small saucepan of water to the boil. Add rocket, return to the boil; drain immediately. Rinse rocket under cold water; drain. Blend rocket with oil until smooth.

prep + cook time 35 minutes
makes 48
tips We used corn kernels from 2 large fresh corn cobs in this recipe, but you can use frozen (then thawed) kernels or well-drained canned kernels. Roast your own capsicum under the griller, or in the oven until the skin blisters and blackens, cover, cool, then remove skin before using. Or, buy roasted capsicum from a deli, or in jars. A lightly oiled non-stick frying pan is ideal for cooking the fritters.

Make-ahead tips
1 week Cook fritters, cool; wrap and freeze.
Last Reheat frozen fritters in a single layer on oven trays, cover loosely with foil, in an oven preheated to 180°C/160°C fan-forced, for about 10 minutes. Make rocket puree close to serving, it will discolour on standing; cover surface of puree with plastic wrap.

12 uncooked medium
    king prawns (540g)
¼ small (250g) cauliflower
175g broccolini
50g green beans
1 small red capsicum (150g)
vegetable oil, for deep-frying
ponzu dipping sauce
1 tablespoon mirin
1 tablespoon rice vinegar
¼ cup (60ml) prepared
    dashi stock
2 tablespoons japanese
    soy sauce
2 teaspoons lime juice
tempura batter
1 cup (150g) plain flour
1 cup (250ml) iced water
½ cup small ice cubes
2 tablespoons sesame seeds

1 Make ponzu dipping sauce.
2 Shell and devein prawns, leaving tails intact. Trim and chop vegetables into bite-sized pieces.
3 Make tempura batter.
4 Heat oil in wok, deep-fryer or deep, wide saucepan to 180°C. Dip prawns and vegetables into batter, one piece at a time (see page 110); wipe off excess batter against edge of bowl, lower carefully into oil. Deep-fry, in batches, for about 30 seconds or until cooked through. Drain on absorbent paper.
5 Serve tempura immediately with ponzu dipping sauce.
ponzu dipping sauce Bring mirin, vinegar, stock and sauce to the boil in small saucepan. Reduce heat, simmer 2 minutes; cool. Stir in juice.
tempura batter Combine flour and the water in medium bowl. Using chopsticks, mix in ice and seeds. Batter should be light and slightly lumpy.

prep + cook time 40 minutes
makes 60
Make-ahead tips
24 hours Ponzu dipping sauce can be made a day ahead; cool, add juice, cover and refrigerate.
8 hours Prepare prawns and vegetables, cover, refrigerate; bring to room temperature before frying.
Last Deep-fry tempura as close as possible to serving time.

tempura with ponzu dipping sauce

manhattan

Place 1 maraschino cherry into chilled
120ml martini glass; rub the cut edge
of an orange over the rim of the glass.
Place ½ cup ice cubes, 45ml whiskey,
15ml sweet vermouth and dash of
angostura bitters in a mixing glass;
stir gently. Strain into glass.

prep time 5 minutes **serves** 1

tom collins

Place 60ml gin, 80ml lemon juice,
2 teaspoons pure icing sugar and
80ml soda water into chilled ice-
filled 340ml highball glass; stir
gently. Garnish with maraschino
cherry and curls of lemon peel.
prep time 5 minutes **serves** 1

33

trio of indian dips

carrot pickle

2 teaspoons vegetable oil
½ teaspoon cumin seeds
½ teaspoon brown
  mustard seeds
2 large carrots (360g),
  grated coarsely
2 tablespoons white
  wine vinegar
1 fresh small red chilli,
  chopped finely
2 teaspoons white sugar
¼ cup (60ml) water

1 Heat oil in small frying pan;
cook seeds, stirring, until
they pop.
2 Add remaining ingredients to
pan; bring to the boil. Reduce
heat; simmer, uncovered, about
15 minutes or until carrot is soft.
makes 1 cup (275g)

dhal

2 tablespoons vegetable oil
1 small brown onion (80g),
  chopped finely
1 clove garlic, crushed
2cm piece fresh ginger (10g),
  grated
½ teaspoon brown
  mustard seeds
¾ cup (150g) red lentils
1½ cups (375ml) water
½ cup (125ml) coconut milk
1 medium tomato (150g),
  chopped finely
2 fresh small green chillies
2 stems fresh curry leaves
  (about 20 leaves)
1 tablespoon lime juice

1 Heat oil in medium saucepan;
cook onion, garlic, ginger and
seeds until fragrant.
2 Add lentils, the water, coconut
milk, tomato, chilli and leaves;
bring to the boil. Reduce heat;
simmer, uncovered, 15 minutes
or until lentils are tender.
3 Stir in juice. Discard chillies
and curry leaves.
makes 2 cups (700g)

coriander mint chutney

2 cups firmly packed fresh
  coriander leaves
1 cup firmly packed fresh
  mint leaves
1 teaspoon white sugar
2 teaspoons white wine vinegar
½ cup (125ml) greek-style
  yogurt
1 tablespoon water

1 Blend or process ingredients
until smooth.
makes 1 cup (200g)

prep + cook time 1 hour
serves 24
tips Serve dips with pappadam
pieces for scoops. Break
pappadams into small pieces
before cooking, either by deep-
frying in hot vegetable oil, or by
microwaving. Season the dips
with salt to suit your taste.
Make-ahead tips
24 hours Make dips; cover,
refrigerate.
Last Cook pappadams, following
package instructions.

green papaya rice paper rolls

150g thin dried rice noodles
  (vermicelli)
½ large (600g) green papaya,
  cut into matchsticks
1 large carrot (180g),
  cut into matchsticks
125g cherry tomatoes,
  chopped coarsely
375g packet 22cm round
  rice paper wrappers (30)
75 large fresh mint leaves
dressing
1 clove garlic, crushed
2 fresh long green chillies,
  chopped finely
2 tablespoons grated
  palm sugar
2 tablespoons fish sauce
½ cup (125ml) lime juice

1 Place noodles in heatproof bowl; cover with boiling water. Stand about 10 minutes or until noodles soften; drain. Cool.
2 Meanwhile, make dressing.
3 Combine noodles, papaya, carrot, tomatoes and dressing in large bowl.
4 Cover bench with a large tea towel. Working with one rice paper wrapper at a time, dip into bowl of warm water for about 15 seconds or until wrapper is soft and pliable; place on tea towel. Place rounded tablespoons of filling in the lower third of the wrapper, top with 3 mint leaves, roll wrapper over the filling to enclose, tuck in the sides, then continue to roll up firmly (see page 110). Cut each roll in half. Repeat with remaining rice paper wrappers, filling and mint leaves. Refrigerate until ready to serve.
dressing Using mortar and pestle, grind garlic and chillies until crushed. Add sugar, sauce and juice; grind until smooth.

prep time 1 hour
makes 60
tip Use a mandolin or V-slicer to cut the papaya and carrot into matchsticks.
Make-ahead tips
8 hours Make rolls; refrigerate. Store loosely packed, with damp paper towel or baking paper between layers as rolls can stick together.

300g chicken thigh fillets,
  cut into 2cm cubes
1 tablespoon kecap manis
½ teaspoon white sugar
1cm piece fresh ginger (5g),
  grated
½ teaspoon fish sauce
1 fresh long red chilli,
  chopped finely
pickled cucumber
¼ cup (60ml) rice vinegar
½ teaspoon salt
2 teaspoons white sugar
4 lebanese cucumbers (520g)

1 Combine chicken, kecap manis, sugar, ginger and sauce in large bowl. Cover; refrigerate 30 minutes.
2 Meanwhile, make pickled cucumber.
3 Cook chicken in large oiled frying pan over medium heat until golden brown and cooked through.
4 Top each cucumber slice with a piece of warm chicken; sprinkle with a little chilli. Serve immediately.
pickled cucumber Stir vinegar, salt and sugar in medium bowl until sugar is dissolved. Cut unpeeled cucumbers into 1cm thick slices. Using teaspoon or melon-baller, remove about half the seeds from each slice to allow space for the chicken pieces (see page 110). Add cucumber to vinegar mixture, stand 10 minutes; drain on absorbent paper.

prep + cook time 40 minutes
makes 30
Make-ahead tips
24 hours Prepare and marinate chicken mixture.
8 hours Slice cucumber; cover, refrigerate.
Last Pickle cucumber slices. Cook chicken.

sticky chicken with pickled cucumber

mini chicken katsu

4 chicken breast fillets (800g)
⅔ cup (100g) plain flour
3 cups (150g) japanese
   breadcrumbs (panko)
3 eggs
vegetable oil, for deep-frying
sauce
⅓ cup (80ml) tonkatsu sauce
1 tablespoon japanese
   soy sauce
1 tablespoon mirin

1 Place chicken breasts between sheets of plastic wrap. Using meat mallet, pound chicken until 1cm thick. Cut chicken into 3cm squares.
2 Place flour and breadcrumbs in separate large shallow bowls. Beat eggs lightly in another large shallow bowl. Coat chicken in flour; shake away excess. Dip chicken in egg, then in breadcrumbs.
3 Make sauce.
4 Heat oil in wok or wide deep saucepan; cook chicken, in batches, until browned and cooked through; drain on a fine wire rack placed over a tray.
5 Serve chicken hot with sauce for dipping.
sauce Bring ingredients to the boil in a small saucepan. Reduce heat; simmer, uncovered, 2 minutes.

prep + cook time 40 minutes
makes 80
Make-ahead tips
24 hours Crumb chicken; place in single layer on tray; cover and refrigerate. Make sauce; cover and refrigerate.
Last Fry chicken close to serving time. Reheat sauce.

margarita

Rub lime slice around rim of 150ml margarita glass; turn glass upside-down and dip wet rim into saucer of salt. Place 1 cup ice cubes, 45ml dark tequila, 30ml cointreau, 30ml lime juice and 30ml sugar syrup (see page 112) in cocktail shaker; shake vigorously. Strain into glass. Garnish with lime slice and curl of lime rind made using a zester.

prep time 5 minutes | **serves** 1

whiskey sour

Chill 180ml stemmed glass. Place
1 cup ice cubes, 45ml rye whiskey,
30ml lemon juice and 15ml sugar syrup
(see page 112) in cocktail shaker; shake
vigorously. Strain into glass. Garnish
with lemon slice and maraschino cherry.
prep time 5 minutes **serves** 1

beef with yorkshire puds & horseradish cream

2 teaspoons vegetable oil
1 clove garlic, crushed
600g piece beef eye fillet
⅓ cup (80ml) vegetable oil, extra
72 sprigs watercress
yorkshire puds
1¾ cups (255g) plain flour
4 eggs
1 cup (250ml) milk
¾ cup (180ml) water
horseradish cream
200g crème fraîche
2 tablespoons horseradish
  cream

1 Preheat oven to 200°C/180°C fan-forced.
2 Combine oil and garlic in small bowl, rub all over beef, cover; stand beef 30 minutes.
3 Meanwhile, make yorkshire pud batter and horseradish cream.
4 Heat heavy medium baking dish on stove top, brown beef over high heat, until browned all over. Transfer beef to oven, roast uncovered, about 15 minutes or until beef is cooked. Remove from oven, cover beef loosely with foil; rest at least 15 minutes before slicing thinly.
5 Increase oven temperature to about 250°C/230°C fan-forced. Drop about ¼ teaspoon vegetable oil into each hole of two 12-hole patty pans.
6 Heat pans in oven for 3 minutes. Remove pans from oven, pour 2 teaspoons batter into each hole. Return pans to oven, cook puds about 10 minutes or until puffed and browned. Repeat with remaining batter.
7 Top each pud with a little horseradish cream, a slice of beef and a sprig of watercress. Arrange on platters; serve immediately.

yorkshire puds Sift flour into medium bowl; make a well in centre. Break eggs into well, gradually stir in milk and water, beat until batter is smooth.
horseradish cream Combine crème fraîche and horseradish cream in small bowl.

prep + cook time 1 hour
makes 72
tip Beef fillet cut from the neck end is best for this recipe.
Make-ahead tips
1 week Bake, cool, wrap and freeze yorkshire puds.
6 hours Roast beef; rest, slice, cover and refrigerate. Bring to room temperature before serving. Make horseradish cream; cover, refrigerate.
Last To reheat, place on oven trays in a single layer, reheat from frozen at 200°C/180°C fan-forced for about 5 minutes. Assemble just before serving.

fennel grissini with prosciutto

2 cups (300g) plain flour
½ teaspoon white sugar
1 teaspoon cooking salt
1 teaspoon dried yeast
2 teaspoons fennel seeds
1 cup (250ml) water,
   approximately
cooking-oil spray
sea salt
20 slices prosciutto (300g)

1 Sift flour, sugar and cooking salt into medium bowl, stir in yeast, seeds and enough of the water to make a soft dough. Turn dough onto floured surface, knead about 5 minutes or until dough is smooth and elastic.
2 Place dough in large oiled bowl, cover with plastic wrap; stand in warm place about 1 hour or until dough is doubled in size.
3 Preheat oven to 220°C/200°C fan-forced. Oil oven trays.
4 Turn dough onto floured surface, knead until smooth. Divide dough into four portions, cut each portion into 15 pieces; roll each piece into a long thin stick (see page 110).
5 Place sticks on oven trays, coat lightly with cooking oil spray. Sprinkle with sea salt.
6 Bake grissini about 15 minutes or until crisp.
7 Meanwhile, cut each prosciutto slice lengthways into three. Wrap a strip around each warm grissini. Serve immediately.

prep + cook time 1 hour
makes 60
Make-ahead tips
1 week Make grissini; store in an airtight container.
8 hours Cut prosciutto into strips; cover, refrigerate.
Last Reheat grissini on oven trays in 200°C/180°C fan-forced oven for about 5 minutes.

1 tablespoon vegetable oil
1 medium brown onion (150g),
  chopped finely
2 cloves garlic, crushed
2 teaspoons ground cumin
½ teaspoon ground allspice
500g lamb mince
1 cup (70g) stale breadcrumbs
⅓ cup (80ml) iced water
1 tablespoon vegetable oil,
  extra

tomato relish
1 tablespoon vegetable oil
1 medium brown onion (150g),
  chopped finely
2 cloves garlic, crushed
1 teaspoon cumin seeds
½ teaspoon ground allspice
½ teaspoon chilli powder
1 teaspoon white sugar
2 tablespoons tomato paste
420g can diced tomatoes

1 Heat half the oil in large frying pan; cook onion and garlic until soft. Stir in spices. Transfer mixture to large heatproof bowl; cool 10 minutes. Using your hand, mix in lamb, breadcrumbs and the water. Roll heaped teaspoons of mixture into balls.
2 Make tomato relish.
3 Heat extra oil in large frying pan; cook meatballs, in batches, until browned and cooked through. Place in tomato relish, reheat gently. Serve meatball mixture in tiny bowls with forks or toothpicks.
tomato relish Heat oil in large saucepan; cook onion and garlic until soft. Stir in spices, sugar, paste and undrained tomatoes; bring to the boil. Reduce heat; simmer, uncovered, 15 minutes.

prep + cook time 40 minutes
makes 60
Make-ahead tips
1 month Make meatballs and relish; freeze.
24 hours Thaw meatballs and relish in refrigerator overnight.
Last Reheat meatballs in 180°C/160°C fan-forced oven and relish in saucepan, or both can be reheated separately in microwave oven.

spicy meatballs with tomato relish

cool as a cucumber

Place ⅓ cup coarsely chopped unpeeled cucumber into cocktail shaker. Using muddler (see page 110), crush cucumber. Add 45ml gin, 30ml lemon juice, 15ml sugar syrup (see page 112) and 1 cup crushed ice; shake vigorously. Strain into chilled 120ml martini glass. Garnish with extra shaved cucumber. **prep time** 5 minutes **serves** 1

bloody mary

Place 1 cup ice cubes, 60ml vodka, 10ml lemon juice, ½ teaspoon prepared horseradish, ¼ teaspoon tabasco, dash worcestershire sauce, pinch celery salt and 150ml vegetable juice or tomato juice in 340ml highball glass; stir gently. Garnish with cracked black pepper and 1 trimmed celery stalk. **prep time** 5 minutes **serves** 1

51

4 duck breasts (600g)
1 teaspoon sea salt
¼ teaspoon ground white
    pepper
1 teaspoon five-spice powder
citrus salsa
1 ruby-red grapefruit (350g)
2 medium oranges (480g)
1 fresh small green chilli,
    chopped finely
1 tablespoon fish sauce
2 tablespoons finely chopped
    fresh coriander leaves

1 Score duck skin in a diagonal pattern (see page 110).
2 Combine salt, pepper and spice in small bowl; rub into both sides of duck.
3 Place duck, skin-side down, in large cold frying pan; place pan over medium heat. Cook about 6 minutes or until skin is crisp and browned. Turn duck, cook 2 minutes. Transfer duck to absorbent-paper-lined plate, cover duck loosely with foil; stand 10 minutes.
4 Make citrus salsa.
5 Slice duck thinly, place each slice in bowl of a serving spoon. Top each duck slice with about ½ teaspoon citrus salsa.
citrus salsa Segment grapefruit and oranges (see page 111); chop finely. Drain over small bowl; reserve juice. Place fruit in medium bowl with chilli, sauce, coriander and 2 tablespoons of reserved juice; toss to combine.

prep + cook time 30 minutes
makes 60
Make-ahead tips
24 hours Rub duck breasts with five-spice mix, cover; refrigerate. Remove duck from refrigerator 30 minutes before cooking.
8 hours Make citrus salsa; cover, refrigerate.
Last Cook duck up to 30 minutes before serving.

duck with citrus salsa

lamb cutlets with dukkah

24 french-trimmed lamb
  cutlets (1.2kg)
1 tablespoon olive oil
dukkah
1 teaspoon cumin seeds
2 teaspoons coriander seeds
2 tablespoons sesame seeds
⅓ cup (45g) roasted hazelnuts
¼ cup (40g) whole blanched
  almonds
1 teaspoon salt
½ teaspoon ground black
  pepper
½ teaspoon sweet paprika

1 Make dukkah.
2 Brush cutlets with oil, cook on preheated char-grill or barbecue over high heat, about 3 minutes each side. Transfer to a warm plate; cover, stand 5 minutes.
3 Spread dukkah onto large plate. Press one side of each hot cutlet onto dukkah just before serving.
dukkah Dry-fry seeds separately in small frying pan until fragrant. Cool. Dry-fry nuts in same pan, stirring, until golden. Cool. Using mortar and pestle (see page 110), grind seeds coarsely; add nuts, grind coarsely. Stir in salt, pepper and paprika.

prep + cook time 35 minutes
makes 24
Make-ahead tips
1 month Make dukkah; store in airtight container in refrigerator.
Last Cook cutlets just before serving.

300g pork mince
400g medium green prawns,
    shelled, deveined,
    chopped coarsely
1.5cm piece fresh ginger, grated
1 clove garlic, quartered
1 fresh small red chilli,
    chopped coarsely
2 green onions, chopped coarsely
¼ cup (60ml) chinese cooking
    wine (shao hsing)
1½ tablespoons light soy sauce
1 teaspoon white sugar
1 egg white
40 wonton wrappers

1 Process pork mince, prawns, ginger, garlic, chilli and onion until finely minced. Add wine, soy, sugar and egg white; process until combined.
2 Place wonton wrappers on bench; place rounded teaspoons pork mixture in centre of each wrapper. Brush a little water around edges of each wrapper; bring edges together to seal (see page 111).
3 Drop wontons, in batches, into a large saucepan of boiling water; boil about 5 minutes or until filling is cooked through. Remove wontons from water with slotted spoon.
4 Serve wontons with soy sauce for dipping.

prep + cook time 40 minutes
makes 40
tip Ponzu dipping sauce (see page 6) would make a good dipping sauce for these wontons.
Make-ahead tips
1 week Make wontons; freeze in a single layer. Transfer frozen wontons to an airtight container; freeze until required.
Last Cook frozen wontons as directed in step 3, for about 10 minutes.

pork & prawn wontons

caipiroska

Cut 1 lime into eight wedges; place into cocktail shaker. Using muddler (see page 110), crush lime wedges with 2 teaspoons caster sugar. Add 45ml vodka and ½ cup crushed ice; shake vigorously. Pour into 260ml old-fashioned glass. Garnish with a curl of lime rind made using a zester. **prep time** 5 minutes **serves** 1

mojito

Cut 1 lime into quarters; place 3 lime wedges into cocktail shaker. Using muddler (see page 110), crush lime wedges with 15ml sugar syrup (see page 112) and 6 sprigs fresh mint. Add 45ml white rum and ½ cup ice cubes; shake vigorously. Strain into 320ml highball glass; top with 150ml soda water. Garnish with remaining lime wedge and mint leaves. **prep time** 5 minutes **serves** 1

lamb rogan josh with rösti

2 teaspoons vegetable oil
1 medium brown onion (150g),
   chopped finely
1 clove garlic, crushed
1.5cm piece fresh ginger,
   grated
600g lamb backstrap, trimmed,
   chopped finely
2 tablespoons rogan josh
   curry paste
2 medium tomatoes (300g),
   seeded, chopped finely
2 tablespoons lemon juice
2 tablespoons finely chopped
   fresh coriander leaves
rösti
2 medium potatoes (400g)
40g butter, melted

1 Make rösti.
2 Meanwhile, heat half the oil in large frying pan; cook onion, garlic and ginger, stirring, until onion is soft. Remove from pan.
3 Add remaining oil to pan; cook lamb until browned. Return onion mixture to pan with paste; cook, stirring, until fragrant. Remove pan from heat. Stir in tomatoes, juice and coriander.
4 Divide lamb mixture into rösti cases; serve immediately.
rösti Place unpeeled potatoes in medium saucepan, cover with cold water, cover pan; bring to the boil. Boil about 20 minutes or until potatoes are almost tender; drain, cool and peel. Coarsely grate potatoes into medium bowl; stir in butter. Preheat oven to 250°C/230°C fan-forced. Press 1 teaspoon potato mixture over base and half-way up side of each hole in two 24-hole mini muffin pans (see page 111). Bake rösti about 10 minutes or until browned around the edges. Remove rösti from oven, stand 30 seconds; remove from pans, drain on absorbent paper.

prep + cook time 1 hour
makes 48
tips We used desiree potatoes, (a thin-skinned red potato) for the rösti. There is no need to oil muffin pans, unless they are scratched.
Make-ahead tips
1 month Cook lamb mixture (don't add tomatoes etc); freeze.
24 hours Thaw lamb mixture overnight in refrigerator.
Last Make rösti up to 2 hours ahead. Reheat lamb mixture in saucepan, add tomatoes etc as above.

beef & stilton pies

2 tablespoons vegetable oil
500g stewing beef,
   cut into 1cm cubes
1 medium brown onion (150g),
   chopped finely
1 clove garlic, crushed
2 tablespoons tomato paste
1 tablespoon plain flour
¼ cup (60ml) dry red wine
2 cups (500ml) beef stock
5 sheets shortcrust pastry
100g stilton cheese, crumbled
1 egg
1 tablespoon milk

1 Heat half the oil in medium saucepan; cook beef in batches until browned. Heat remaining oil in same pan; cook onion and garlic until soft.
2 Return beef to pan with paste, stir over heat until combined. Add flour; cook, stirring until mixture bubbles. Stir in wine, then gradually stir in stock; continue stirring until mixture boils and thickens. Reduce heat; simmer, covered, about 45 minutes or until beef is tender. Cool.
3 Meanwhile, cut 48 x 6.5cm rounds as close together as possible from all the pastry sheets; line two 24-hole mini (1 tablespoon) muffin pans. Prick the base of each pastry case with a fork.
4 Preheat oven to 220°C/200°C fan-forced.
5 Fill each case with rounded teaspoons of beef mixture; top with a small piece of cheese.

6 Cut out 48 x 4.5cm rounds from remaining pastry scraps. Combine egg and milk in a small bowl; brush around inside top edge of each pastry case with egg mixture, cover with pastry rounds, press edges together. Brush pies with more egg mixture; cut a hole in each pie to allow steam to escape.
7 Bake pies about 20 minutes or until golden. Stand pies in pan 5 minutes before serving.

prep + cook time 1¾ hours
makes 48
tips Any beef cut suitable for stewing can be used for the pie filling: gravy beef, skirt, blade or chuck steak. Trim all sinew and tissue before cooking.
Make-ahead tips
1 month Bake pies, cool, wrap and freeze.
24 hours Thaw pies in refrigerator overnight.
Last Reheat pies in a single layer on oven trays, covered loosely with foil, in oven at 180°C/160°C fan-forced about 10 minutes.

tom kha gai

250g chicken tenderloins
1½ cups (375ml) water
1½ cups (375ml) chicken stock
400ml coconut milk
2cm piece fresh ginger (10g), peeled, sliced thinly
10cm stick fresh lemon grass (20g), bruised
4 fresh kaffir lime leaves, torn
1 fresh small red chilli, halved lengthways
¼ cup finely chopped fresh coriander root
2 teaspoons fish sauce
1 teaspoon grated palm sugar
1 tablespoon lime juice
50g straw mushrooms, sliced thinly
3 fresh kaffir lime leaves, shredded finely, extra
2 fresh small red chillies, chopped finely, extra

1 Half-fill a medium frying pan with water, add chicken; bring to the boil. Reduce heat; simmer, covered, about 5 minutes or until chicken is tender. Drain chicken, discard liquid. Chop chicken finely.

2 Meanwhile, place the water, stock, half the coconut milk, ginger, lemon grass, lime leaves, chilli, coriander and sauce in medium saucepan; bring to the boil. Reduce heat; simmer 15 minutes.

3 Strain liquid; discard solids. Return liquid to same pan with remaining coconut milk, sugar, juice, chicken and mushrooms. Reheat, without boiling.

4 Divide soup into small (about ½ cup (125ml) capacity) bowls; sprinkle with extra lime leaves and chillies.

prep + cook time 45 minutes
serves 12
tips Use any cut of chicken you like for poaching, such as breast or thigh fillets. We used tenderloins because they're quicker to cook. Use a good-flavoured chicken stock for this recipe; if you like, use the chicken poaching liquid in place of some of the measured water in the recipe. Use scissors to finely shred kaffir lime leaves.
Make-ahead tips
24 hours Prepare soup ingredients, cover and refrigerate.
Last Soup is best made just before serving.

2 teaspoons olive oil
½ small red onion (50g),
  chopped finely
¼ small red capsicum (40g),
  chopped finely
1 chipotle chilli in adobo sauce,
  drained, seeded,
  chopped finely
⅓ cup (80ml) tomato pasta sauce
1 cup (160g) finely shredded
  barbecued chicken
5 x 20cm flour tortillas
vegetable oil, for shallow-frying
¼ cup (60g) sour cream
48 fresh coriander leaves

1 Heat olive oil in medium frying pan. Cook onion and capsicum, stirring, about 2 minutes or until soft. Add chilli and pasta sauce, cook, stirring, until sauce thickens slightly. Remove from heat, stir in chicken. Cover to keep warm.
2 Cut 48 x 4cm rounds from tortillas.
3 Heat vegetable oil in a small frying pan; fry two tortilla rounds at a time until browned lightly. Drain on absorbent paper. While tacos are still warm and pliable, fold in half, place on a tray; place a wooden spoon on top to stop them unfolding while they cool (see page 111).
4 Divide chicken mixture into taco shells; top with sour cream and coriander. Serve immediately.

prep + cook time 1 hour
makes 48
tip You need the meat from about half a barbecued chicken for this recipe.
Make-ahead tips
8 hours Cook tortillas and fold into taco shells. Cook chicken mixture; cover, refrigerate.
Last Reheat chicken mixture in saucepan or microwave. Reheat taco shells on a tray, uncovered, in 200°C/180°C fan-forced oven for about 30 seconds, this makes them pliable enough to fill easily. Fill tacos just before serving.

chicken chipotle tacos

piña colada

Blend 1 cup ice cubes, 30ml white rum,
30ml dark rum, 80ml pineapple juice,
20ml sugar syrup (see page 112), 40ml
coconut cream and dash angostura
bitters until smooth. Pour into 400ml
tulip-shaped glass. Garnish with
pineapple piece and leaves.
prep time 5 minutes **serves** 1

champagne side-car

Place 20ml brandy, 20ml cointreau, 20ml lemon juice and 15ml sugar syrup (see page 112) in chilled 230ml champagne flute glass; stir gently. Top with 150ml chilled dry white sparkling wine. Garnish with strawberry slices.

prep time 5 minutes **serves** 1

sticky pork on betel leaves

1.2kg pork belly, skin and
  bones removed
⅓ cup (80ml) fish sauce
2 tablespoons grated
  palm sugar
1 star anise
1cm piece fresh ginger (5g),
  peeled, sliced thinly
2 cloves garlic, bruised
1 litre (4 cups) water
vegetable oil, for deep-frying
1½ teaspoons white
  peppercorns
½ cup coarsely chopped
  fresh coriander root
8 green onions, chopped coarsely
½ cup (90g) grated palm sugar,
  extra
¼ cup (60ml) fish sauce, extra
48 betel leaves
4 fresh kaffir lime leaves,
  shredded finely

1 Cut pork into 1cm cubes. Place
pork in medium saucepan with
sauce, sugar, star anise, ginger,
garlic and the water; bring to
the boil. Reduce heat; simmer,
covered, about 25 minutes or
until pork is tender. Drain pork;
discard liquid and spices. Dry
pork well with absorbent paper
2 Heat oil in wok, deep-fryer or
deep wide saucepan; deep-fry
pork, in batches, until golden
brown. Drain on absorbent paper.
3 Meanwhile, dry-fry peppercorns
in small frying pan until fragrant.
Using mortar and pestle (see
page 110), grind peppercorns
until fine. Add coriander and
onion, grind until smooth. Add
extra sugar and extra sauce;
grind until sugar is dissolved.
4 Stir-fry pork with coriander
mixture in oiled wok or large
frying pan over high until pork
is crisp.
5 Place betel leaves on a serving
platter, top with pork mixture
and lime leaves.

prep + cook time 55 minutes
makes 48
tips Use a splatter guard while
deep-frying pork; these are
handy to have and are available
from supermarkets. The pork
becomes sticky during the
second cooking (stir-frying),
so use a non-stick pan to make
cleaning up easier. Use scissors
to finely shred kaffir lime leaves.
Make-ahead tips
1 week Deep-fry pork; cool,
then freeze.
24 hours Thaw pork in
refrigerator overnight.
Last Stir-fry pork, assemble as
close to serving time as possible.

40 wonton wrappers
cooking-oil spray
1 chinese barbecued duck
8 fresh lychees (200g), peeled,
  sliced thinly
1 cup lightly packed fresh
  coriander leaves
2 fresh small red chillies,
  sliced thinly
4 green onions, sliced thinly
dressing
¼ teaspoon five-spice powder
1 teaspoon honey
2 teaspoons chinese
  black vinegar
1 tablespoon light soy sauce
1 tablespoon hot water
few drops sesame oil

1 Preheat oven to 220°C/200°C
fan-forced. Coat 40 holes of two
24-hole mini (1 tablespoon) muffin
pans with cooking-oil spray.
2 Cut a 7.5cm round from each
wonton wrapper; line each pan
hole with a wonton round (see
page 111). Coat wrappers lightly
with oil spray. Bake cases about
7 minutes or until golden brown
around the edges.
3 Meanwhile, remove meat
and skin from duck, reserve
separately; chop meat finely
and slice skin thinly.
4 Place skin on baking-paper-
lined oven tray; bake about
10 minutes or until crisp. Drain
on absorbent paper.
5 Make dressing.
6 Place duck meat and skin
in medium bowl with lychees,
coriander, chilli, onion and
dressing; toss gently to combine.
Divide mixture into cases. Serve
immediately.
dressing Combine ingredients
in a small bowl.

prep + cook time 1 hour
makes 40
Make-ahead tips
1 week Bake wonton cases;
store in an airtight container.
8 hours Prepare filling
ingredients.
Last Make filling. Fill cases just
before serving.

duck & lychee wonton cases

french kiss

Place 30ml chambord (black raspberry liqueur)
and 30ml berry iced tea in chilled 230ml
champagne saucer; stir gently. Top with 120ml
chilled lemonade. Garnish with fresh raspberries.
prep time 5 minutes **serves** 1 **tip** We used
'forest berry' tea bags to make the iced tea.

adam's apple

Rub lime slice around rim of 150ml martini glass;
turn glass upside-down and dip wet rim into
saucer of cinnamon sugar. Place 1 cup ice cubes,
30ml vanilla vodka, 30ml green apple vodka,
120ml apple juice, 20ml sugar syrup (see page
112) and 20ml lime juice in cocktail shaker; shake
vigorously. Strain into glass. Garnish with fanned
apple slices. **prep time** 5 minutes **serves** 1

chicken tandoori with naan bread

1 cup (280g) yogurt
⅓ cup finely chopped fresh
  coriander leaves
400g chicken breast fillets,
  cut into 1cm cubes
2 tablespoons tandoori paste
⅓ cup (110g) mango chutney
naan bread
2 cups (300g) plain flour
¼ teaspoon baking powder
¼ teaspoon salt
1 teaspoon dried yeast
1 teaspoon kalonji seeds
⅓ cup (95g) yogurt
1 tablespoon vegetable oil
1 egg
⅓ cup (80ml) warm milk,
  approximately

1 Combine yogurt and coriander in large bowl; reserve and refrigerate ¼ cup for serving. Stir chicken and paste into remaining coriander yogurt; refrigerate.
2 Meanwhile, make naan bread.
3 Stir chicken mixture in heated oiled frying pan until cooked.
4 Top each naan with ¼ teaspoon mango chutney, a piece of the tandoori chicken and a dollop of reserved coriander yogurt.
naan bread Sift flour, baking powder and salt into large bowl; stir in yeast and seeds. Make a well in centre; add yogurt, oil, egg and enough milk to mix to a soft dough. Turn dough onto floured surface, knead 5 minutes or until smooth and elastic. Place dough in large oiled bowl; cover, stand in warm place 2 hours or until doubled in size. Preheat grill to highest setting. Heat a heavy-duty oven tray under grill. Cut dough in half and working with one half at a time, divide dough into 2cm balls. Roll balls out to 3mm thick, stretch ends of each piece of dough (see page 111). Grill naan, in batches, on hot tray, 45 seconds each side or until browned.

prep + cook time 1 hour
(+ standing)
makes 80
Make-ahead tips
1 week Cook naan breads; cool, wrap and freeze.
24 hours Make coriander yogurt. Combine the chicken, paste and coriander yogurt; cover, refrigerate.
4 hours Thaw naan breads at room temperature.
Last Cook chicken mixture. Reheat naan breads on oven trays, covered loosely with foil, in oven at 220°C/200°C fan-forced. Assemble naan breads just before serving.

1 teaspoon olive oil

½ teaspoon sesame oil

500g uncooked large prawns, shelled, deveined, chopped finely

1 small avocado (200g), chopped finely

2 medium tomatoes (300g), seeded, chopped finely

2 tablespoons sweet chilli sauce

2 teaspoons fish sauce

2 tablespoons finely chopped fresh coriander leaves

1 tablespoon lime juice

30 fillo or shortcrust pastry cases (see pages 108 & 109)

30 fresh coriander leaves, extra

1 Heat oils in medium frying pan; cook prawns, stirring, over medium heat until changed in colour. Transfer prawns to heatproof bowl; cool.

2 Add avocado, tomato, sauces, chopped coriander and juice to prawns; mix gently.

3 Divide prawn mixture into pastry cases, top with extra coriander leaves.

prep + cook time 35 minutes
makes 30
Make-ahead tips
4 hours Cook prawns; prepare remaining ingredients.
Last Combine filling ingredients; fill pastry cases just before serving.

prawn, avocado & sweet chilli tarts

oysters three ways

oysters with bloody mary granita

1¾ cups (375ml) canned
   vegetable juice
¼ cup (60ml) vodka
¼ teaspoon smoked paprika
½ teaspoon celery salt
1 tablespoon lemon juice
few drops tabasco sauce
48 oysters on the half shell

1 Combine vegetable juice,
vodka, paprika, salt, lemon juice
and sauce in shallow cake pan.
Cover; freeze several hours or
overnight.
2 Scrape granita into long shards
with a fork, spoon over oysters.
Serve immediately.

prep time 10 minutes (+ freezing)
makes 48
Make-ahead tips
24 hours Make granita.
Last Assemble oysters and
granita just before serving.

oysters with shallot & chilli vinegar

2 shallots (50g), chopped finely
1 fresh long red chilli,
   chopped finely
½ cup (125ml) white wine
   vinegar
48 oysters on the half shell

1 Combine shallots, chilli and
vinegar in small bowl; stand
20 minutes.
2 Top oysters with vinegar
mixture. Serve immediately.

prep time 10 minutes
(+ standing)
makes 48
Make-ahead tips
8hrs Make shallot and chilli
vinegar; cover, refrigerate.
Last Assemble oysters just
before serving.

oysters with green apple sorbet

4 medium green-skinned apples
   (600g), chopped coarsely
1 lebanese cucumber (130g),
   chopped coarsely
1½ tablespoons lemon juice
¼ cup (60ml) glucose syrup
48 oysters on the half shell

1 Using an electric juice
extractor, juice apples and
cucumber. Combine juice
and glucose in medium jug;
refrigerate 1 hour. Using an
ice-cream machine, churn
sorbet until firm; freeze.
2 Top oysters with tiny scoops
of sorbet. Serve immediately.

prep time 45 minutes
(+ refrigerator & freezing)
makes 48
Make-ahead tips
1 week Make and freeze sorbet.
12 hours Place scoops of
sorbet on trays; freeze.
Last Assemble oysters and
sorbet just before serving.

long island iced tea

Place ½ cup ice cubes, 15ml vodka, 15ml white rum, 15ml white tequila, 15ml gin, 10ml cointreau, 15ml lemon juice and 15ml sugar syrup (see page 112) in cocktail shaker; shake vigorously. Pour into ice-filled 250ml highball glass. Top with 80ml cola; garnish with lemon slice. **prep time** 5 minutes **serves** 1

bellini

Place 45ml peach nectar, 15ml peach schnapps and 5ml lime juice in chilled 230ml champagne flute glass; stir gently. Top with 150ml chilled dry white sparkling wine. Garnish with a peach wedge. **prep time** 5 minutes **serves** 1

lobster, herb & tomato on witlof

2 uncooked lobster tails (500g)
1 tablespoon olive oil
40g butter
2 shallots (50g), chopped finely
1 clove garlic, crushed
½ teaspoon mustard powder
2 teaspoons finely grated
   lemon rind
1 tablespoon lemon juice
1 medium tomato (150g),
   seeded, chopped finely
2 tablespoons finely chopped
   fresh flat-leaf parsley
2 tablespoons finely chopped
   fresh chervil
48 red witlof leaves

1 Using scissors, cut along sides of the soft skin on the lobster belly (see page 111). Peel away skin, remove meat from the shell. Cut into 5mm cubes.
2 Heat 1 teaspoon of the oil and 10g of the butter in medium frying pan, add lobster; cook, stirring, over medium heat, until changed in colour.
3 Add remaining oil and butter to same pan; cook shallot and garlic until soft. Remove pan from heat; stir in mustard, rind, juice, lobster, tomato and herbs.
4 Divide lobster mixture into witlof leaves. Serve immediately.

prep + cook time 45 minutes
makes 48
tips The same weight of prawns can be used instead of lobster. You will need about 6 witlof for this recipe.
Make-ahead tips
8 hours Prepare lobster for cooking. Prepare filling ingredients; cover, refrigerate.
Last Cook lobster and complete the filling; fill leaves just before serving.

2 medium tomatoes (300g),
  peeled, seeded, chopped finely
1 tablespoon olive oil
1 tablespoon verjuice
2 tablespoons fresh chervil
  leaves
2 teaspoons finely grated
  lemon rind
24 scallops on the half shell
pea puree
1½ cups (180g) frozen peas
¼ cup (60ml) cream
2 tablespoons hot water,
  approximately

1 Make pea puree.
2 Combine tomato, oil, verjuice,
chervil and rind in medium bowl.
3 Remove scallops from shells;
wash and dry shells. Divide pea
puree into shells.
4 Heat large oiled frying pan;
cook scallops about 30 seconds
each side or until browned lightly
but still soft in the centre.
5 Place scallops on pea puree;
top scallops with tomato
mixture. Serve immediately.
pea puree Boil, steam or
microwave peas until tender;
drain. Blend peas with cream
and enough of the water to give
a thick pouring consistency.

prep + cook time 30 minutes
makes 24
tip Use plain peas, not minted
peas for this recipe.
Make-ahead tips
8 hours Make pea puree;
cover, refrigerate. Make tomato
mixture.
Last Place pea puree in shells
about 30 minutes before cooking
scallops as close to serving
as possible.

seared scallops with pea puree & tomato

smoked salmon sushi
with pickled green onion

1½ cups (300g) sushi rice
  (koshihikari)
2¼ cups (560ml) water
⅓ cup (80ml) rice wine vinegar
1½ teaspoons white sugar
1½ teaspoons salt
2 tablespoons mirin
2 sheets nori
1 tablespoon wasabi paste
400g thinly sliced smoked
  salmon
japanese soy sauce, for dipping
pickled green onion
3 green onions, sliced thinly
  lengthwise
¼ cup (60ml) rice wine vinegar
¼ cup (60ml) water
1 teaspoon white sugar
½ teaspoon salt

1 Rinse rice under cold water until water runs clear. Place rice and the water in medium heavy-based saucepan over high heat; bring to the boil. Reduce heat; simmer, covered, 12 minutes. Remove rice from heat; stand, covered, 10 minutes.
2 Tip rice into large wide bowl. Using a flat wooden spoon or spatula, cut and slice the combined vinegar, sugar, salt and mirin through the rice (see page 111).
3 Line 19cm x 30cm lamington pan with plastic wrap extending 5cm over long sides of pan. Trim and position nori sheets to cover base of pan in single layer. Press rice over nori. Spread wasabi over rice. Top wasabi with single layer of salmon; press down gently. Cover pan; refrigerate until ready to serve.
4 Make pickled green onion.
5 Lift sushi from pan to chopping board; using large, heavy, wet knife, cut sushi into 4cm squares. Top sushi squares with drained pickled onion. Serve with japanese soy sauce for dipping.

pickled green onion Combine ingredients in medium bowl; cover, refrigerate at least 1 hour to allow onions to curl.

prep + cook time 1½ hours
makes 35
tip Wet hands before pressing the rice over nori in pan, this will help prevent the rice sticking.
Make-ahead tips
24 hours Make pickled green onions; cover, refrigerate.
8 hours Prepare sushi ready for cutting; cover, refrigerate before serving.

rosy cheeks

Place ½ cup ice cubes, 30ml campari, 5ml grenadine syrup and ¼ teaspoon rosewater in cocktail shaker; shake vigorously. Pour into ice-filled 250ml highball glass. Top with 160ml lemonade. Garnish with fresh rose petals. **prep time** 5 minutes **serves** 1

italian orange blossom

Place 1 cup ice cubes, 45ml orange juice, 30ml white sambuca,
15ml tequila and 10ml lemon juice in cocktail shaker;
shake vigorously. Strain into chilled 230ml martini glass.
prep time 5 minutes **serves** 1

okonomiyaki (tiny japanese pancakes)

½ cup (75g) plain flour
½ cup (75g) self-raising flour
tiny pinch bicarbonate of soda
3 eggs
½ cup (125ml) water
2 teaspoons japanese soy sauce
300g uncooked large king
    prawns, shelled, deveined,
    chopped finely
1 cup (50g) finely chopped
    wombok
3 green onions, chopped finely
¼ cup (55g) japanese
    mayonnaise
1 tablespoon tonkatsu sauce
¼ sheet nori, shredded finely

1 Sift flours and soda into medium bowl. Make well in centre; whisk in eggs, water and sauce to make a smooth batter.
2 Stir prawns, wombok and onion into batter.
3 Cook teaspoons of batter, in batches, in large oiled frying pan over medium heat until bubbles appear. Turn pancakes to cook other side. Place on wire rack to cool.
4 Top each pancake with ¼ teaspoon mayonnaise, a drop of tonkatsu and a sprinkling of nori. Serve immediately.

prep + cook time 35 minutes
makes 40
tip Use scissors to finely shred the nori.
Make-ahead tips
8 hours Make pancakes; cover, refrigerate. Bring pancakes to room temperature 30 minutes before serving.
Last Assemble pancakes just before serving.

200g piece yellowfin tuna
cooking-oil spray
150g unpeeled kipfler potatoes
100g green beans
1 large tomato (220g), seeded
2 eggs, hard-boiled
1 tablespoon olive oil
2 teaspoons balsamic vinegar
½ teaspoon wholegrain mustard
3 drained anchovy fillets,
   chopped finely
1 tablespoon rinsed drained
   baby capers, chopped finely
2 tablespoons finely grated
   parmesan cheese
2 tablespoons finely chopped
   fresh flat-leaf parsley
36 shortcrust pastry cases
   (see page 108)

1 Coat tuna with cooking-oil spray. Heat medium frying pan over high heat; cook tuna about 45 seconds each side. Remove from pan; cover.
2 Cut potatoes into 3mm cubes. Boil, steam or microwave potato until tender; drain. Slice beans thinly; boil, steam or microwave beans until tender. Drain.
3 Chop tomato, egg white and tuna the same size as potatoes. Finely grate egg yolk or push through a sieve.
4 Combine oil, vinegar, mustard, anchovy, capers, cheese and parsley in medium bowl. Add chopped ingredients; mix gently.
5 Divide niçoise mixture into pastry cases; sprinkle each with egg yolk. Serve immediately.

prep + cook time 30 minutes
makes 36

tips Use sashimi quality tuna; the loin is the best cut for this recipe. A non-stick pan is best to use for cooking the tuna. Don't overcook the tuna, it should be rare.
Make-ahead tips
8 hours Make filling; cover, refrigerate.
Last Fill pastry cases just before serving.

tuna niçoise tarts

wasabi salmon

650g piece salmon fillet
2 teaspoons wasabi paste
¼ cup (60ml) japanese soy sauce
½ teaspoon sesame oil
dipping sauce
⅓ cup (80ml) rice wine vinegar
1 tablespoon white sugar
½ lebanese cucumber (65g),
   seeded, chopped finely

1 Using tweezers, remove fine bones from salmon. Remove skin; cut salmon into 2cm cubes.
2 Combine paste, sauce and oil in medium bowl, add salmon; turn to coat, stand 15 minutes.
3 Meanwhile, make dipping sauce.
4 Drain salmon; discard marinade. Heat large oiled frying pan; cook salmon, in batches, over high heat about 20 seconds each side. Serve salmon with dipping sauce.
dipping sauce Stir ingredients in small bowl until sugar dissolves.

prep + cook time 35 minutes (+ standing)
makes 48
tips A non-stick pan is best to use for cooking the salmon. Don't overcook the salmon, it should be rare.
Make-ahead tips
8 hours Chop salmon, prepare marinade, prepare sauce.
Last Marinate salmon, cook just before serving; serve warm.

sunday mojito

Cut ½ lime into quarters; place into cocktail shaker. Using muddler (see page 110), crush lime with 2 lychees and 6 sprigs fresh mint. Add 45ml malibu, 15ml lychee liqueur and ½ cup ice cubes; shake vigorously. Strain into cocktail glass; top with 80ml pineapple juice. Garnish with pineapple leaf and orchid. **prep time** 5 minutes **serves** 1

strawberry & peach tequila popsicles

Blend or process 3 medium peaches until smooth. Push peaches through a sieve into a medium bowl; stir in 2 tablespoons grated palm sugar, 40ml tequila, 20ml cointreau and 20ml lemon juice. Divide half the peach mixture into 12 x ⅓ cup (80ml) paddle pop moulds (or paper cups); reserve remaining peach mixture. Freeze popsicles about 30 minutes or until surface is firm. Meanwhile, blend or process 500g coarsely chopped strawberries until smooth. Push strawberries through a sieve into a medium bowl; stir in 2 tablespoons grated palm sugar and 40ml tequila. Press paddle pop stick firmly into each popsicle. Divide half the strawberry mixture into moulds; reserve remaining strawberry mixture. Freeze popsicles about 30 minutes or until surface is firm. Divide remaining peach mixture into moulds; freeze popsicles about 30 minutes or until surface is firm. Divide remaining strawberry mixture into moulds; freeze overnight.
prep time 30 minutes (+ freezing) **makes** 12

1 cup (90g) rolled oats
100g cold butter,
   chopped coarsely
½ cup (75g) wholemeal
   plain flour
2 tablespoons plain flour
¼ teaspoon bicarbonate of soda
1½ tablespoons brown sugar
1 tablespoon milk
200g cheddar cheese
fig jam
3 large fresh figs (240g),
   chopped finely
2 tablespoons caster sugar
1 teaspoon finely grated
   orange rind
2 tablespoons orange juice

1 Make fig jam.
2 Preheat oven to 170°C/150°C fan-forced. Grease oven trays.
3 Process oats until chopped finely. Add butter and sifted dry ingredients; pulse until crumbly. Add milk; process until mixture comes together. Turn dough onto floured surface, knead gently until smooth.
4 Divide dough in half; roll each half between sheets of baking paper until 3mm thick. Cut dough into 3cm squares. Using spatula, carefully place oat cakes on trays.
5 Bake oat cakes 10 minutes or until golden brown. Cool on trays 5 minutes; transfer to wire racks to cool completely. Serve oat cakes topped with jam and a small piece of cheese.
fig jam Stir ingredients in small saucepan over low heat for about 10 minutes or until thick; cool. Transfer jam to small bowl; cover, refrigerate.

prep + cook time 45 minutes
makes 80
tip Buy a good strong-tasting mature cheddar cheese to go with the oat cakes and jam.
Make-ahead tips
1 week Make jam; cover, refrigerate. This fig jam is not a true jam that will keep from season to season. Make oat cakes; store in an airtight container.
Last If oat cakes soften, re-crisp in the oven for a few minutes, just before serving. Assemble just before serving.

oat cakes with cheddar & fig jam

smoked trout with pickled onion on rye

1 teaspoon hot english mustard
1 teaspoon lemon juice
½ cup (120g) sour cream
200g hot-smoked trout
2 x 250g packets thinly sliced
   dark rye bread
bunch fresh dill
pickled onion
½ small red onion (50g),
   quartered, sliced thinly
¼ cup (60ml) white wine vinegar
2 teaspoons white sugar
½ teaspoon salt

1 Make pickled onion.
2 Combine mustard, juice and cream in small bowl.
3 Discard skin and bones from trout; flake flesh into medium bowl.
4 Spread each slice of bread with mustard mixture; cut each slice into 6 squares.
5 Top each square with trout, drained pickled onion and a sprig of dill. Serve immediately.
pickled onion Place ingredients in screw-top jar; shake well. Refrigerate several hours or overnight.

prep time 30 minutes
(+ refrigeration)
makes 96
tips A whole smoked rainbow trout will give you enough flesh for this recipe. Smoked salmon can be used in place of trout.
Make-ahead tips
24 hours Skin, bone and flake trout. Prepare pickled onion. Make sour cream spread; cover, refrigerate.
1 hour Assemble ready to serve.

caramelised onion
& goats cheese quiches

48 shortcrust pastry cases
  (see page 108)
1 tablespoon olive oil
20g butter
2 large brown onions (400g),
  quartered, sliced thinly
3 teaspoons fresh lemon
  thyme leaves
4 eggs, beaten lightly
⅔ cup (160ml) milk
120g firm goats cheese,
  crumbled

1 Preheat oven to 200°C/180°C
fan-forced. Return baked pastry
cases to mini muffin pans.
2 Heat oil and butter in medium
frying pan. Add onion, reduce
heat; cook, covered, stirring
occasionally, about 20 minutes,
or until onion is caramelised.
Remove from heat; stir in thyme.
3 Divide onion mixture into
pastry cases.
4 Combine eggs and milk in
large jug; pour into pastry cases,
sprinkle with cheese.
5 Bake quiches about 10 minutes
or until filling is set.

prep + cook time 50 minutes
makes 48
tip These quiches are best
served warm.
Make-ahead tips
2 days Cook caramelised onion;
cover, refrigerate.
24 hours Prepare filling
ingredients; cover, refrigerate.
1 hour Fill pastry cases and
bake quiches.

smoked chicken
& asparagus quiches

48 shortcrust pastry cases
  (see page 108)
5 medium asparagus spears (85g)
250g smoked chicken,
  chopped finely
2 tablespoons finely chopped
  fresh chives
4 eggs
⅔ cup (160ml) milk
½ cup (40g) finely grated
  parmesan cheese

1 Preheat oven to 200°C/180°C
fan-forced. Return baked pastry
cases to mini muffin pans.
2 Divide asparagus, chicken
and chives into pastry cases.
3 Combine eggs and milk in
large jug; pour into pastry cases,
sprinkle with cheese.
4 Bake quiches about 10 minutes
or until filling is set.

prep + cook time 30 minutes
makes 48
tip These quiches are best
served warm.
Make-ahead tips
24 hours Prepare filling
ingredients.
1 hour Fill pastry cases and
bake quiches.

watermelon cosmo

Place 1 cup ice cubes, 45ml vodka, 30ml triple sec, 60ml chilled watermelon juice and 20ml lime juice in cocktail shaker; shake vigorously. Strain into chilled 230ml martini glass. Garnish with watermelon wedges and lime peel.
prep time 5 minutes **serves** 1

elderflower fizz
Place ½ cup ice cubes, 30ml elderflower cordial, 30ml gin, 20ml lemon juice and 250ml soda water into chilled 450ml highball glass; stir gently. Garnish with sliced lemon. **prep time** 5 minutes **serves** 1

shortcrust cases

2 cups (300g) plain flour
175g cold butter,
   chopped coarsely
1 egg yolk
2 teaspoons iced water,
   approximately

1 Process flour and butter until crumbly. With motor operating, add egg yolk and enough water to make ingredients barely come together.
2 Turn dough onto floured surface, knead gently until smooth. Cut pastry in half, shape into rectangles, enclose in plastic wrap; refrigerate 30 minutes.
3 Grease two 24-hole mini (1 tablespoon) muffin pans.
4 Roll out one portion of pastry on floured surface or between sheets of baking paper until 2mm thick. Cut out 24 x 6.5cm rounds; gently press pastry rounds into holes of one pan. Prick bases of cases well with a fork. Refrigerate 20 minutes. Repeat with remaining pastry and muffin pan.
5 Meanwhile, preheat oven to 230°C/210°C fan-forced.
6 Bake chilled cases about 10 minutes or until crisp. Stand cases 5 minutes, before transferring to wire racks to cool.

prep + cook time 30 minutes (+ refrigeration)
makes 48
tip Re-roll pastry scraps only once; excess handling and rolling will result in tough pastry cases.
Make-ahead tips
1 week Bake pastry cases; store in airtight containers.
1 hour If cases soften, re-crisp in 180°C/160°C fan-forced oven for about 5 minutes.

pastry cases

bought cases

There are many different types, shapes and sizes of pastry cases available. Some supermarkets stock a small range, but you're more likely to find these cases in specialty food shops and delis.

fillo cases

12 sheets fillo pastry
125g butter, melted
cooking-oil spray

1 Preheat oven to 230°C/210°C fan-forced.
2 Place one sheet pastry on bench, brush lightly, but evenly with butter. Top with another sheet of pastry, brush with more butter. Repeat process until there are 4 sheets of pastry stacked together, finish with butter. Repeat with remaining pastry and butter until you've got three stacks of buttered pastry. Cut out 48 x 7cm rounds from the pastry stacks.

3 Push pastry rounds, butter-side down, into two 24-hole mini (1 tablespoon) muffin pans. Coat pastry lightly with cooking-oil spray.
4 Bake cases about 5 minutes or until crisp. Cool in pans 5 minutes before turning onto wire racks to cool.

prep + cook time 30 minutes
makes 48
Make-ahead tips
1 week Bake pastry cases; store in airtight containers.
1 hour Re-crisp cases in 180°C/160°C fan-forced oven for about 3 minutes.

using a mortar & pestle
Place the ingredients to be ground in the mortar (the bowl). Use the pestle to pound and grind the ingredients until they're as fine as needed. Coarse ingredients like whole seeds and peppercorns might need to be broken down and ground first before adding finer ingredients to be ground.

shredding basil leaves
Stack about 10 (more if you can manage them) basil leaves on top of each other, roll up the leaves lengthways, as tightly as possible. Using a sharp knife, cut the roll of leaves crossways as finely as possible – this is called "to chiffonnade". This technique minimises bruising and darkening of basil and mint leaves.

muddling
Use a wooden muddler (see also page 115) to gently squash and mix ingredients together, use a gentle pounding then circular action when using a muddler. The muddler will bruise the rinds of citrus fruits, which releases the natural oils into the mixture.

battering tempura
Using long chopsticks, working quickly and as close to the wok of heated oil as possible, hold one piece of food in the chopsticks, sweep the food through the batter. Wipe off the excess batter against the side of the bowl and gently lower the food into the hot oil.

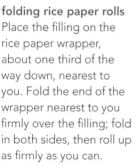

folding rice paper rolls
Place the filling on the rice paper wrapper, about one third of the way down, nearest to you. Fold the end of the wrapper nearest to you firmly over the filling; fold in both sides, then roll up as firmly as you can.

making cucumber cups
Slice unpeeled cucumbers into 1cm thick slices. Use a small melon baller or a small teaspoon – like a coffee spoon – to scoop out about half the seeds from each cucumber slice, without breaking through. This makes a small cavity (or cup) to hold the filling.

shaping grissini
Divide the dough into quarters. Working with one quarter at a time, cut 15 even-sized pieces from the dough. Roll each piece of dough on a lightly floured surface into a long stick about 18cm long. Place sticks on oiled oven trays.

scoring duck skin
Using a very sharp knife, cut just through the skin to the fatty layer beneath, on each of the duck breasts, in a diagonal pattern.

110

segmenting oranges
Peel oranges thickly, to remove all white pith. Hold an orange over a bowl to catch the juice. Using a sharp knife, cut down (but not all the way through) close to the membrane that divides one orange segment, then cut down, next to the membrane on the other side of the same segment. The segment will come away easily. Repeat with remaining segments.

making wontons
Place wonton wrappers on the bench, top with the filling then brush or dab water around the outside edges of each wrapper. Pull all four corners together in the centre and pinch the points together to seal each wonton.

making mini rösti
Cook, cool and peel potatoes, then grate coarsely. Press 1 teaspoon of the potato mixture evenly over the base and half way up the side of each of 48 mini (1 tablespoon) muffin pan holes.

making mini tacos
Shallow-fry two 4cm tortilla rounds at a time, then drain on an absorbent-paper-lined flat tray. While the tortillas are still warm, fold each one in half then weight them with a wooden spoon to stop them unfolding. Leave the tacos to cool to room temperature.

making wonton cases
Coat 40 holes of two 24-hole mini (1 tablespoon) muffin pans with cooking-oil spray. Cut a 7.5cm round from one wonton wrapper, gently press the round into one pan hole – the wrapper will fold and pleat, but that's fine. Repeat with remaining wonton wrappers.

shaping mini naan
Working with half the dough, tear off 2cm balls from the dough – you should have 20 pieces. Work each piece into a smooth ball, then roll or press each piece out flat to an oval shape about 3mm thick. Stretch both ends of each piece of dough. Grill naan in batches. Repeat with remaining dough.

preparing lobster
Hold the lobster tail belly-side up in one hand. Use sharp scissors to cut down both sides of the soft skin of the belly; discard the skin. Pull the shell back from the flesh and remove the flesh in one piece.

making sushi rice
Place the cooked rice into a large bowl. Using a flat wooden spoon or rubber or plastic spatula, cut and slice the combined liquid ingredients as evenly as possible through the rice.

sugar syrup

Stir 1 cup (220g) caster sugar with 1 cup (250ml) water in small saucepan over low heat, until sugar dissolves; bring to the boil. Reduce heat; simmer, uncovered, 5 minutes. Cool. Refrigerate in an airtight container for up to 1 month. **prep + cook time** 10 minutes **makes** 350ml

drink garnishes

1 Strawberry slice ice cubes **2** Skewered halved lemon slices **3** Skewered blueberries
4 Finely sliced star fruit **5** Skewered rockmelon balls **6** Seedless watermelon heart

glasses

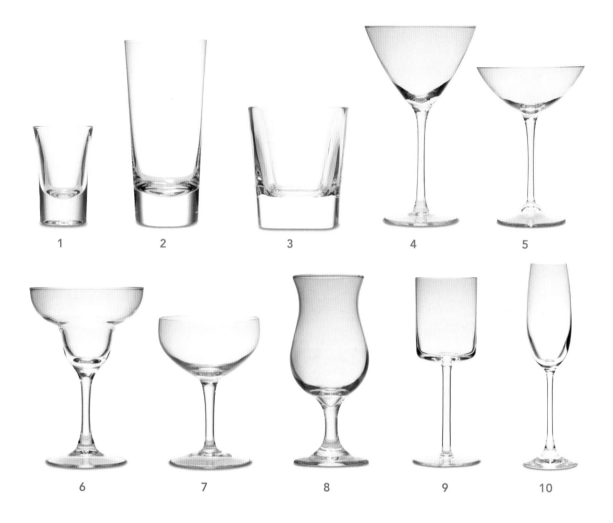

1 Shot glass **2** Highball glass **3** Old-fashioned glass **4** Martini glass **5** Champagne saucer
6 Margarita glass **7** Cocktail glass **8** Tulip glass **9** Stemmed glass **10** Champagne flute

bar equipment

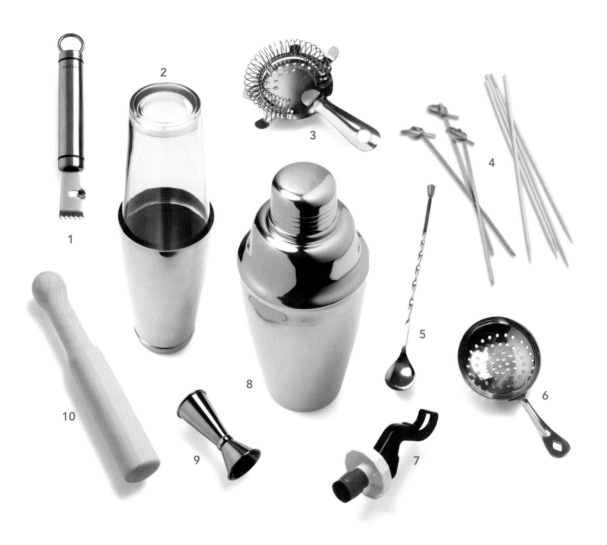

1 Zester **2** Cocktail shaker **3** Hawthorn strainer **4** Skewers **5** Long-handled mixing spoon **6** Ice scoop
7 Bottle sealer or stopper **8** Cocktail shaker with strainer/lid **9** Jigger (one & two nip measures) **10** Muddler

glossary

allspice also called pimento or jamaican pepper. Available whole or ground.

almonds flat, pointy-tipped nuts having a pitted brown shell enclosing a creamy white kernel which is covered by a brown skin; there are two types, sweet and bitter, with the former being the most readily available and most used in cooking.

baking powder a raising agent consisting mainly of two parts cream of tartar to one part bicarbonate of soda.

betel leaves grown and consumed in India and throughout South-East Asia, betel leaves are used raw as a wrap, cooked as a vegetable, or chopped and used as both a herb and a medicine. They are available at some greengrocers and most Asian food stores, especially those specialising in Vietnamese produce.

bicarbonate of soda also known as baking soda.

breadcrumbs

japanese also known as panko; available in larger pieces and fine crumbs. Has a lighter texture than Western-style breadcrumbs. Available from Asian food shops and some supermarkets, and unless you make rather coarse breadcrumbs from stale white bread that's either quite stale or gently toasted, nothing is an adequate substitution.

packaged prepared fine-textured but crunchy white breadcrumbs; good for coating or crumbing foods to be fried.

broccolini a cross between broccoli and Chinese kale; long asparagus-like stems with a long loose floret, both completely edible. Resembles broccoli in look but is milder and sweeter in taste.

butter we use salted butter unless stated otherwise; 125g is equal to 1 stick (4 ounces).

buttermilk originally the term given to the slightly sour liquid left after butter was churned from cream, today it is commercially made similarly to yogurt. Sold alongside fresh milk products in supermarkets. Despite the implication of its name, buttermilk is low in fat.

capers the grey-green buds of a warm climate (usually Mediterranean) shrub, sold either dried and salted or pickled in a vinegar brine; baby capers are also available both in brine or dried in salt.

capsicum also called bell pepper.

cheese

fetta a Greek crumbly textured goat- or sheep-milk cheese with a sharp, salty taste. Ripened and stored in salted whey.

fontina a smooth, firm Italian cow-milk cheese with a creamy, nutty taste and red or brown rind; ideal for melting or grilling.

goats made from goat milk, has an earthy, strong taste. Available in soft, firm and crumbly textures, various shapes and sizes, and also rolled in ash or herbs.

gouda a hard cheese with a creamy texture and nutty flavour. Originally produced in Holland, it is now made in several other countries. If not available, use Edam which is similar but not as creamy.

haloumi a Greek Cypriot cheese with a semi-firm, spongy texture and very salty yet sweet flavour. Ripened and stored in salted whey; it's best grilled or fried, and holds its shape when heated. Eat warm as it becomes tough and rubbery on cooling.

mozzarella soft, spun-curd cheese from southern Italy and traditionally made from water-buffalo milk. Now generally made from cow milk, it is the most popular pizza cheese due to its low melting point and elasticity when heated.

parmesan also called parmigiano; a hard, grainy cow-milk cheese originating in Parma, Italy. The curd for this cheese is salted in brine for a month before being aged for up to 2 years, preferably in humid conditions. Reggiano is the best and made only in Emilia-Romagna, Italy.

chilli

chipotle pronounced cheh-pote-lay. The name used for jalapeño chillies once dried and smoked. Having a deep, intensely smoky flavour, rather than a searing heat, chipotles are dark brown, almost black in colour and wrinkled in appearance. Chipotle chillies are also available in adobo sauce, purchased in cans, from specialty food shops and delicatessens. If unavailable, soak dried chipotle chillies in hot water for about 20 minutes or until soft, then drain. They won't be as soft as the canned product but will impart a smoky flavour.

powder the Asian variety is the hottest, made from dried ground thai chillies; can be used instead of fresh chillies in the proportion of ½ teaspoon chilli powder to 1 medium chopped fresh red chilli.

chinese barbecued duck traditionally cooked in special ovens in China; dipped into and brushed during roasting with a sticky sweet coating made from soy sauce, sherry, ginger, five-spice, star anise and hoisin sauce. Available from Asian food shops as well as dedicated chinese barbecued meat shops.

coconut milk not the liquid found inside the fruit (coconut water), but the diluted liquid from the second pressing of the white flesh of a mature coconut (the first pressing produces coconut cream). Available in cans and cartons at most supermarkets.

crème fraîche a mature, naturally fermented cream (minimum fat content 35 per cent) having a velvety texture and slightly tangy, nutty flavour. Crème fraîche, a French variation of sour cream, can boil without curdling and can be used in both sweet and savoury dishes.

cumin also known as zeera or comino; resembling caraway in size, cumin is the dried seed of a plant related to the parsley family. Has a spicy, almost curry-like flavour. Available dried as seeds or ground.

dashi the basic fish and seaweed stock that makes the distinctive flavour of many Japanese soups and casserole dishes.

Made from dried bonito (a type of tuna) flakes and kombu (kelp); instant dashi (dashi-no-moto) is available as powder, granules and liquid concentrate from Asian food shops.

fennel also known as finocchio or anise; a crunchy green vegetable slightly resembling celery that's eaten raw in salads; fried as an accompaniment; or used as an ingredient in soups and sauces. Also sometimes the name given to the dried seeds of the plant which have a stronger licorice flavour.

fish sauce called naam pla (Thai-made) and nuoc naam (Vietnamese); the two are almost identical. Made from pulverised salted fermented fish (often anchovies); has a pungent smell and strong taste. Available in varying degrees of intensity, so use according to your taste.

flour

chickpea (besan) also called gram; made from ground chickpeas so is gluten-free and high in protein. Used in Indian cooking to make dumplings, noodles and chapati; for a batter coating for deep-frying; and as a sauce thickener.

plain also called all-purpose flour.

self-raising all-purpose plain or wholemeal flour with baking powder and salt added; make at home in the proportion of 1 cup plain flour to 2 teaspoons baking powder.

ginger, fresh also called green or root ginger; the thick gnarled root of a tropical plant. Can be kept, peeled, covered with dry sherry in a jar and refrigerated, or frozen in an airtight container.

hazelnuts also known as filberts; plump, grape-size, rich, sweet nut with a brown inedible skin that is removed by rubbing heated nuts together vigorously in a tea-towel. Hazelnut meal is made by grounding the hazelnuts to a coarse flour.

horseradish a vegetable having edible green leaves but mainly grown for its long, pungent white root. Occasionally found fresh in specialty greengrocers and some Asian food shops, but commonly purchased in bottles at the supermarket in two forms: prepared horseradish and horseradish cream. These cannot be substituted one for the other in cooking but both can be used as table condiments. Horseradish cream is a commercially prepared creamy paste consisting of grated horseradish, vinegar, oil and sugar, while prepared horseradish is the preserved grated root.

kaffir lime leaves also known as bai magrood, look like they are two glossy dark green leaves joined end to end, forming a rounded hourglass shape. Used fresh or dried in many South East Asian dishes, they are used like bay leaves or curry leaves, especially in Thai cooking. Sold fresh, dried or frozen, the dried leaves are less potent so double the number if using them as a substitute for fresh; a strip of fresh lime peel may be substituted for each kaffir lime leaf.

kalonji seeds also called nigella or black onion seeds; are angular seeds, black on the outside and creamy within, having a sharp nutty flavour.

kecap manis a dark, thick sweet soy sauce used in most South East Asian cuisines. The sauces's sweetness is derived from the addition of either molasses or palm sugar when brewed. Use as a condiment, dipping sauce, ingredient or marinade.

kipfler potatoes small, finger-shaped, nutty flavour; great baked and in salads.

lebanese cucumbers short, slender and thin-skinned. Probably the most popular variety because of its tender, edible skin, tiny, yielding seeds, and sweet, fresh and flavoursome taste.

lemon grass also called takrai, serai or serah. A tall, clumping, lemon-smelling and tasting, sharp-edged aromatic tropical grass; the white lower part of the stem is used, finely chopped, in much of South East Asian cuisine. Can be found, fresh, dried, powdered and frozen, in supermarkets and greengrocers as well as Asian food shops.

lychees a small fruit from China with a hard shell and sweet, juicy flesh. The white flesh has a gelatinous texture and musky, perfumed taste. Discard the rough skin and seed before using in salads or as a dessert fruit. It is also available canned in a sugar syrup.

nori a type of dried seaweed used in Japanese cooking as a flavouring, garnish or for sushi. Sold in thin sheets, plain or toasted (yaki-nori).

mayonnaise we use whole-egg mayonnaise unless specified.

japanese is made with rice vinegar, giving it a slightly different flavour to most commercial mayonnaises; is also usually thinner in texture. Can be purchased from Asian grocers.

mirin a Japanese champagne-coloured cooking wine, made of glutinous rice and alcohol. It is used expressly for cooking and should not be confused with sake. A seasoned sweet mirin, manjo mirin, made of water, rice, corn syrup and alcohol, is used in Japanese dipping sauces.

mushrooms

button small, cultivated white mushrooms with a mild flavour. When we call for an unspecified type of mushroom, use button.

straw also known as paddy straw or grass mushrooms; seldom available fresh, but easily found canned or dried in Asian grocery stores. A common ingredient in stir-fries, they have an intense earthy flavour.

mustard

dijon also called french. Pale brown, creamy, distinctively flavoured, fairly mild French mustard.

powdered finely ground white (yellow) mustard seeds. Available from most supermarkets.

wholegrain also known as seeded. A French-style coarse-grain mustard made from crushed mustard seeds and dijon-style french mustard. Works well with cold meats and sausages.

oil

olive made from ripened olives. Extra virgin and virgin are the first and second press, respectively, of the olives and are therefore considered the best; the "extra light" or "light" name on other types refers to taste not fat levels.

sesame made from roasted, crushed, white sesame seeds; a flavouring rather than a cooking medium.

vegetable any of a number of oils sourced from plant rather than animal fats.

onions, green also called scallion or (incorrectly) shallot; an immature onion picked before the bulb has formed, having a long, bright-green edible stalk.

paprika ground dried sweet red capsicum (bell pepper); there are many grades and types available, including sweet, hot, mild and smoked.

pork belly fatty cut sold in rashers or a piece, with or without rind or bone.

prosciutto unsmoked Italian ham; salted, air-cured and aged; usually eaten uncooked.

quail eggs very small eggs, with a speckled shell, usually eaten poached or soft- or hard-boiled. Available from good butchers, delicatessens and speciality foods stores.

rocket also called arugula, rugula and rucola; peppery green leaf eaten raw in salads or used in cooking. Baby rocket leaves are smaller and less peppery.

sashimi fish sold as sashimi has to meet stringent guidelines regarding its handling. We suggest you seek local advice from authorities before easting any raw seafood.

sesame seeds black and white are the most common of this small oval seed, however there are also red and brown varieties. Toast the seeds in a heavy-based frying pan over low heat.

soy sauce also called sieu; made from fermented soybeans. Several variations are available in supermarkets and Asian food stores; we use Japanese soy sauce unless indicated otherwise.

japanese an all-purpose low-sodium soy sauce made with more wheat content than its Chinese counterparts; fermented in barrels and aged.

sugar

palm also called nam tan pip, jaggery, jawa or gula melaka; made from the sap of the sugar palm tree. Light brown to black in colour and usually sold in rock-hard cakes; use brown sugar if unavailable.

white coarse, granulated table sugar, also known as crystal sugar.

sumac a purple-red, astringent spice ground from the wild berries of a Mediterranean shrub; adds a tart, lemony flavour to dips and dressings and goes well with barbecued meat. Buy from Middle Eastern food stores.

sushi rice (koshihikari) small, round-grain white rice. If unavailable, use a short-grain rice such as arborio and cook using the absorption method.

tabasco sauce brand-name of an extremely fiery sauce made from vinegar, hot red peppers and salt.

tandoori paste available from most supermarkets; when using commercially available curry pastes, use according to taste.

tonkatsu sauce a Japanese dipping sauce traditionally served with the crumbed pork cutlet dish called tonkatsu. The sauce consists of tomato sauce (ketchup), japanese soy sauce, worcestershire sauce, mustard and sake in varying proportions.

turmeric also called kamin; is a rhizome related to galangal and ginger. Must be grated or pounded to release its acrid aroma and pungent flavour. Known for the golden colour it imparts, fresh turmeric can be substituted with the more commonly found dried powder.

verjuice an acidic juice made from unripe grapes that can be used as an ingredient in sauces, for deglazing or as an alternative to vinegars otherwise used in salad dressings. Available from delicatessens and speciality foods stores.

vinegar

balsamic originally from Modena, Italy, there are now many balsamic vinegars on the market ranging in pungency and quality depending on how, and for how long, they have been aged. Quality can be determined up to a point by price; use the most expensive sparingly.

chinese black is available from most Asian supermarkets, dark in colour; it has a smoky-malt flavour that works well in stir-fries, marinades and Asian-style salad dressings.

red wine made from red wine.

rice a colourless vinegar made from fermented rice and flavoured with sugar and salt. Also called seasoned rice vinegar; sherry can be substituted.

wasabi Asian horseradish used to make the pungent, green-coloured sauce traditionally served with Japanese raw fish dishes; sold in powdered or paste form.

watercress one of the cress family, a large group of peppery greens used raw in salads, dips and sandwiches, or cooked in soups. Highly perishable, so it must be used as soon as possible after purchase.

wonton wrappers also called wonton skins; made of flour, eggs, and water, they come in varying thicknesses. Sold packaged in large amounts and found in the refrigerated section of Asian grocery stores; gow gee, egg or spring roll pastry sheets can be substituted.

worcestershire sauce thin, dark-brown spicy sauce; used as a seasoning for meat, gravies and cocktails, and as a condiment.

yeast a raising agent. Granular (7g sachets) and fresh compressed (20g blocks) yeast can almost always be substituted for each other.

zucchini also called courgette.

index

conversion chart

measures

One Australian metric measuring cup holds approximately 250ml; one Australian metric tablespoon holds 20ml; one Australian metric teaspoon holds 5ml.

The difference between one country's measuring cups and another's is within a two- or three-teaspoon variance, and will not affect your cooking results. North America, New Zealand and the United Kingdom use a 15ml tablespoon.

All cup and spoon measurements are level. The most accurate way of measuring dry ingredients is to weigh them. When measuring liquids, use a clear glass or plastic jug with the metric markings.

We use large eggs with an average weight of 60g.

dry measures

METRIC	IMPERIAL
15g	½oz
30g	1oz
60g	2oz
90g	3oz
125g	4oz (¼lb)
155g	5oz
185g	6oz
220g	7oz
250g	8oz (½lb)
280g	9oz
315g	10oz
345g	11oz
375g	12oz (¾lb)
410g	13oz
440g	14oz
470g	15oz
500g	16oz (1lb)
750g	24oz (1½lb)
1kg	32oz (2lb)

liquid measures

METRIC	IMPERIAL
30ml	1 fluid oz
60ml	2 fluid oz
100ml	3 fluid oz
125ml	4 fluid oz
150ml	5 fluid oz (¼ pint/1 gill)
190ml	6 fluid oz
250ml	8 fluid oz
300ml	10 fluid oz (½ pint)
500ml	16 fluid oz
600ml	20 fluid oz (1 pint)
1000ml (1 litre)	1¾ pints

length measures

METRIC	IMPERIAL
3mm	⅛in
6mm	¼in
1cm	½in
2cm	¾in
2.5cm	1in
5cm	2in
6cm	2½in
8cm	3in
10cm	4in
13cm	5in
15cm	6in
18cm	7in
20cm	8in
23cm	9in
25cm	10in
28cm	11in
30cm	12in (1ft)

oven temperatures

These oven temperatures are only a guide for conventional ovens. For fan-forced ovens, check the manufacturer's manual.

	°C (CELSIUS)	°F (FAHRENHEIT)	GAS MARK
Very slow	120	250	½
Slow	150	275-300	1-2
Moderately slow	160	325	3
Moderate	180	350-375	4-5
Moderately hot	200	400	6
Hot	220	425-450	7-8
Very hot	240	475	9

If you like this cookbook, you'll love these...

  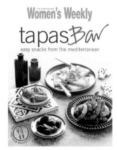

 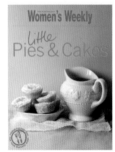 

These are just a small selection of titles available in
The Australian Women's Weekly range on sale at selected
newsagents, supermarkets or online at www.acpbooks.com.au

also available in bookstores...

ACP BOOKS

General manager Christine Whiston
Editor-in-chief Susan Tomnay
Creative director Hieu Chi Nguyen
Art director & designer Hannah Blackmore
Senior editor Stephanie Kistner
Food writer Xanthe Roberts
Food director Pamela Clark
Recipe development Sammie Coryton, Rebecca Squadrito
Sales & rights director Brian Cearnes
Marketing manager Bridget Cody
Senior business analyst Rebecca Varela
Circulation manager Jama Mclean
Operations manager David Scotto
Production manager Victoria Jefferys

ACP Books are published by ACP Magazines a division of
PBL Media Pty Limited

PBL Media, Chief Executive Officer Ian Law
Publishing & sales director, Women's lifestyle Lynette Phillips
Group editorial director, Women's lifestyle Pat Ingram
Marketing director, Women's lifestyle Matthew Dominello
Commercial manager, Women's lifestyle Seymour Cohen
Research director, Women's lifestyle Justin Stone

Produced by ACP Books, Sydney.

Published by ACP Books, a division of ACP Magazines Ltd,
54 Park St, Sydney; GPO Box 4088, Sydney, NSW 2001.
phone (02) 9282 8618; fax (02) 9267 9438.
acpbooks@acpmagazines.com.au; www.acpbooks.com.au

Printed by Toppan Printing Co, China.

Australia Distributed by Network Services,
phone +61 2 9282 8777; fax +61 2 9264 3278;
networkweb@networkservicescompany.com.au
United Kingdom Distributed by Australian Consolidated Press (UK),
phone (01604) 642 200; fax (01604) 642 300; books@acpuk.com
New Zealand Distributed by Netlink Distribution Company,
phone (9) 366 9966; ask@ndc.co.nz
South Africa Distributed by PSD Promotions,
phone (27 11) 392 6065/6/7; fax (27 11) 392 6079/80;
orders@psdprom.co.za
Canada Distributed by Publishers Group Canada
phone (800) 663 5714; fax (800) 565 3770; service@raincoast.com

Title: Cocktails & nibbles / food director Pamela Clark.
ISBN: 978-1-86396-898-0 (pbk.)
Notes: Includes index.
Subjects: Cocktails. Appetizers. Cookery.
Other authors/contributors: Clark, Pamela.
Dewey number: 641.568

© ACP Magazines Ltd 2009
ABN 18 053 273 546

Scanpan cookware is used in the AWW Test Kitchen.

The publishers would like to thank the following for props used in
photography: The Bay Tree; Robert Burton; David met Nicole;
hart & heim; The Hospitality Centre; No Chintz; Orson & Blake; Plenty
Kitchen & Tableware; Potters Paints & Wallpapers; Space Furniture;
Spence & Lyda; Verve Designer collections; Waterford Wedgewood.

To order books, phone 136 116 (within Australia)
or order online at www.acpbooks.com.au
Send recipe enquiries to:
recipeenquiries@acpmagazines.com.au

acp books